YOUNG
Frederick Douglass

Freedom Fighter

First-Start® Biography

by Andrew Woods
illustrated by Allan Eitzen

SCHOLASTIC INC.
New York Toronto London Auckland Sydney
Mexico City New Delhi Hong Kong Buenos Aires

ISBN-13: 978-0-439-87859-3
ISBN-10: 0-439-87859-4

12 11 10 9 8 7 6 5 4 3 2 1   7 8 9 10 11 12/0

Printed in the U.S.A.   23

First Scholastic printing, February 2007

Frederick was born a slave. But he became a great leader who fought for the rights of African-Americans.

Frederick Bailey was born in Maryland
in 1817. His mother was a slave, and her
owner would not let her raise him.
So Fred lived with his grandparents,
Betsey and Isaac Bailey.

Fred was happy. He had fun playing with
his cousins, helping his Grandmama, and
fishing in the river.

Because he was a slave, Fred was only given two knee-length shirts each year. These shirts were all he had to wear in cold winters and hot summers.

When Fred was 7, Grandmama took him
to the plantation of his master, Captain
Anthony. Grandmama did not want to
leave him, but she had no choice. Fred
was scared and lonely.

At the plantation, he helped bring the
cows in for milking. He cleaned the front
yard and ran errands for Captain Anthony.
The work wasn't too hard, but Fred was
always tired and hungry.

Slaves had to wake up before sunrise and did not stop working until after dark. For breakfast, the children ate cornmeal mush from a big bowl. Dinner might be just a piece of cornbread.

One night, the cook did not give Fred any
dinner. Fred sat outside the kitchen, too
hungry to fall asleep. Suddenly he had a
surprise visitor—his mother! She had
traveled from a plantation 15 miles away.

His mother held him and gave him a
ginger cake to eat. Then she told the cook
to treat Fred better. From then on, Fred
knew that his mother loved him and was
always thinking about him.

When Fred was 8, he was sent to Baltimore to work for Captain Anthony's relatives. They were Sophia and Hugh Auld. Fred had to take care of their young son, Tommy. Here he was treated well and had plenty to eat.

Every afternoon, Mrs. Auld read the Bible to Tommy and Fred. Fred loved to listen to the stories. He asked Mrs. Auld to teach him to read.

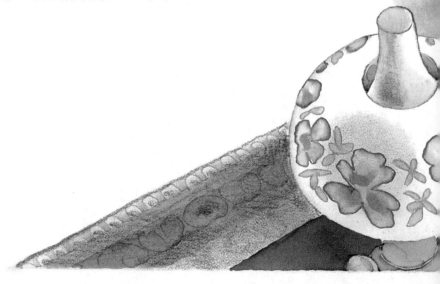

Mrs. Auld was happy to teach him. Fred loved these afternoon lessons. He quickly learned the alphabet and could spell many short words.

One day Mrs. Auld told her husband how fast Fred was learning. Mr. Auld got very angry. He said it was against the law for slaves to learn how to read. Mrs. Auld never gave Fred another lesson.

But Fred still wanted to learn. He took any chance he could to teach himself how to read and write.

In March 1833, Fred was sent back to the plantation. His new master was Thomas Auld, Hugh Auld's brother. He often beat his slaves. He did not like Fred and treated him harshly.

When Fred was 17, Thomas Auld sent him
to the farm of Edward Covey. Covey
promised to turn "trouble-making" slaves
into obedient slaves.

Fred was brave. One day, while Covey was
beating him, Fred fought back and won.

After that, Fred was more determined
than ever to be a free man.

A few years later, Fred was sent back to
Baltimore. There he worked in a shipyard.
He was happier now, but still wanted
to be free.

One day he met a free black sailor. This sailor had papers that proved he was a free man. The sailor lent Fred these papers and a uniform to help him escape to the North, where slavery was illegal.

On September 3, 1838, Fred escaped to
freedom. He took a train to New Bedford,
Massachusetts. And he changed his name
to Frederick Douglass to avoid capture.

In New Bedford, Douglass got a job in a shipyard. Later he married Anna Murray, a free black woman from Baltimore.

Douglass joined a group of abolitionists. They were people who wanted to end slavery. In 1841, he made his first speech against slavery. It was a big hit with the audience.

Over the next four years, Douglass gave many speeches. He wrote a book about his life.

The Aulds read Douglass's book. They became very angry and wanted their runaway slave returned. Douglass went to England so he would not be captured.

In England, Douglass became a popular speaker and writer. He found friends who raised enough money to buy his freedom from the Aulds.

After two years, Douglass returned to the United States and went to Rochester, New York. He started an anti-slavery newspaper called *The North Star.*

When the Civil War began, Douglass asked President Lincoln to let black soldiers fight in the Union Army. Lincoln agreed.

The Civil War ended slavery. But Douglass
continued to fight for civil rights and
freedom for black people until he died
on February 20, 1895.

Frederick Douglass's words led many
people on the path to liberty—

"Freedom for all."